THE GARDEN OF EDEN, KURNA.

IN MESOPOTAMIA

BY

MARTIN SWAYNE, *pseud.*

Maurice Nicoll

ILLUSTRATED BY THE AUTHOR

HODDER AND STOUGHTON

LONDON   NEW YORK   TORONTO

MCMXVII

-1917-

BY THE SAME AUTHOR

———

LORD RICHARD IN THE
   PANTRY
THE SPORTING INSTINCT
CUPID GOES NORTH

HODDER AND STOUGHTON

CONTENTS

IN MESOPOTAMIA

I

THE GATEWAY OF THE GARDEN OF EDEN

THERE is nothing to suggest that you are approaching the gateway of the Garden of Eden when you reach the top of the Persian Gulf, unless the sun be that Flaming Sword which turns every way to keep the way of the Tree of Life. Of cherubim we could see no signs. We lay motionless awaiting orders by wireless. Of the country before us we knew next to nothing. We did not grasp that the great river at whose mouth we lay was called

1

down into the other for hour after hour. A squall arose and the ships had to part company and we lay for two days tossing and rolling in a dun-coloured atmosphere. Then once more we joined up, and the unloading continued of the four hundred tons of equipment, which had already been dumped on shore at Alexandria. It is a costly business bringing out a hospital to these parts. About midday we weighed anchor on the new ship, and crept up the channel over the bar. There were no gas buoys to mark its course, and Fao, which lies near the mouth of the river, had no lighthouse, so night traffic was presumably impossible.

The sudden sight of the belts of palm trees, the occasional square mud dwellings, and the steamy, hot-house look of the banks came as a surprise. Those of us who had been to the Dardanelles had half expected that this end of Turkey would be much like the other—

broken country and sandy scrub, with hills. But here is only a broad swift river, a strip of vivid green verdure, and beyond the immense plain stretching to the horizon. In the stream was a small tug bearing the letters A.P.O.C. At Abadan we saw the big circular tanks of the Anglo-Persian Oil Company where the oil from Ahwaz, which travels through miles of piping, is refined. Above Abadan, which is just a cluster of circular tanks, slender chimneys and square houses on the arid plain, with a mass of barges lining the numerous wharfs, we passed Mohammerah. On the opposite bank —the west bank is called the right bank—you can see the Turkish trenches where they opposed our first advance among the palms at the battle of Sahil on November 16th, 1914, with a force of five thousand men and twelve guns. The ground is intersected with narrow creeks cut for irrigation purposes ; and the trenches

and hold a kind of social parade from which
the suggestion of a slave market was not
entirely absent. There was a continual procession of boats and painted *belums*, the native
gondola, long and narrow, with curved ends,
and either rowed or poled by two *belumchis*.
In them were fair-skinned, unveiled women
with many bangles on their arms, wearing
robes of dark brilliant hues. On the shore,
under the palms, wandered a crowd of white-
robed Arabs, with red or blue turbans. Occasionally one saw a khaki uniform. It was
intensely hot and damp. A haze lay over the
further reaches of the river, and the sky had
a brassy look unlike the intense turquoise
clarity of the Egyptian sky. The palm fronds
seemed metallic. As far as the eye could see
along the right bank lay a confused mass of
low white buildings, tents, huts of yellow
matting and piles of stores. Gangs of Arabs

TOWING ON THE TIGRIS.

of sacking for a sail, and a long pole, managed to reach their destination somehow. It was curious to see these primitive craft filled with the black cases of the precious X-ray plant.

The creeks round Ashar branch off at right angles to the Shatt-el-Arab at intervals of a few hundred yards, and extend for two or three miles inland. They are broad and richly bordered with palms and pomegranate. In places a network of vines festoons the trunks. A yellow tinge in the heart of the palms showed the coming crop of dates. Seen in a picture these creeks are idyllic, winding broad, calm and peaceful through the groves. Slim boats glide up and down them, nut-brown children splash in them, and women, veiled in black, come from the little villages to draw water in brass vessels at their margins with graceful movements.

We landed from a roomy barge with a tug fastened alongside. The men were cheery, and a mouth-organ and a mandoline wafted us on. Something dark and indeterminate swept by on the swift current. It was said to be the body of a dead Turk, bound for the Persian Gulf, after its voyage of two hundred odd miles from Kut. We landed, uncomfortably hot. The men fell in and we prepared to march off. A swarthy Arab, in red and white headgear held in position by two thick rings of camel hair, wearing curved slippers and saffron-coloured robes, stood scowling before us, spitting at intervals. A group of sappers near by seemed unaffected by his behaviour. The scowl and the spitting seem merely habits, induced by the country. But it is necessary to orientate oneself very carefully in the East. A long tramp followed up Dusty Lane, between scorching mud walls. We passed dirty booths,

Singer : " We are doing a great deal of work!"

Chorus : " May Allah reward us ! "

*　　*　　*　　*　　*

The Tommies' refrain was more picturesque.
Imagine six men carrying a crate.

Singer : (Softly) " Is it 'ot ? "   (Pause.)

Chorus : " I don't think ! "

Singer : (Fuller and staccato) " 'Ot as 'ell ? "

Chorus : " I don't think ! " etc.

General Chorus : (repeatedly, with passion).

" Aller, Oller, Aller !

Oh, Aller, Oller, Aller !

Aller, Oller Oo ! "

Bully beef came along in the afternoon, and
we had landed with full water - bottles, for
drinking water was unavailable. Towards
evening some double-roofed tents were run up.
The men settled down in the empty sheds
alongside the creek. We got to bed in a
thunderstorm—a vivid zigzag banging affair

that circled round most of the night. The rain turned the ground into something beyond description as regards its slippery properties. Only a native donkey can keep footing in such ground. There is no road metal available in Mesopotamia. It is a stoneless place. The frogs trumpeted in chorus all night ; packs of dogs or jackals swept about in droves, once at full pelt through our tent, like devils of the storm. It was nightmarish, but sleep brought that wonderful balancing force that sometimes clothes itself in dreams, and steeps the spirit in all that is lacking. Just before falling asleep I reflected that Adam and Eve might well have been excused in such a country.

The urgency of the situation demanded that we should open what wards we could for the reception of sick and wounded at once. We had no nurses, partly because there was no accommodation for them. Four sheds alongside the creek were got in order. Iron bedsteads draped in white, mosquito nets resembling bridal veils, bedside tables, and cupboards arranged themselves in rows. An immense hammering and shouting filled the stifling air. The sheds began to look moderately inviting—neat and clean, smelling faintly of antiseptics which smelt better than the things in the creek. At first about fifty beds were put into each shed; in a short time beds were crowded into every available corner of the clearing. Fresh sheds were being erected by natives. Since the ground was undermined by marsh, the sheds had to be built on piles driven six feet into the spongy soil. There was only one pile driver,

which resembled a cross-section of a lamp post,
and was worked by a fatigue party of wild-
haired Indian troops from Afghanistan regions.
One would have thought from their flashing
eyes when the pile driver crashed home that
they played a secret game in which each
imagined his bitterest enemy was in the place
of the pile.

The problem of water arose at once. There
was no general water supply at that time, and
each unit had to solve its own problem. Our
supply had to come from the creek, which was
thick and turbid and contained a multitude
of unsavoury things. At first it was sedi-
mented with alum, which precipitated the
suspended matter in a gelatinous mass, and the
clear fluid was chlorinated with bleaching
powder. There is only one consolation in
drinking well chlorinated water. You know
that it contains nothing except chlorine. With

seemed impossible to import any new ones, and they cost about sixpence each. Our hospital was situated at a considerable distance from the town. We were not allowed a motor launch, and the roads were often impassable for bullock tongas, owing to the floods which were then prevalent. Soda water was therefore fetched by *belum*. You were poled down the creek to the river, and rowed through the maze of traffic to Ashar creek. Turning out of the broad swift river, up the noisy creek you came on the riverside cafés, built on piles and filled with splenetic-eyed Arabs sipping coffee and various coloured sweet drinks. A cheap gramophone playing a thin Eastern music, may be sounding. The conversation is animated and guttural, constantly interspersed with that hollow, metallic rasp that is like the noise of an engine exhaust. The town is of white mud and stone, with wooden balconies

painted a vivid blue, and flat roofs. A
minaret rises behind it with a blue-tiled
extremity supporting the upraised hand and
crescent. The streets are narrow and airless.
In the shops are a mass of articles of all
descriptions : tinned stuff, tobacco, clocks,
hair-oil, cheap jewellery, odd bottles of doubt-
ful wine, scent, rugs, copper vessels, sweets,
sauces, pickles. Innumerable flies surround
everything. On much of the tinned stuff were
very old labels. No man of experience up-
country in India will touch tinned stuff of that
description. The soda water factory was in a
small courtyard. There was a big green gaso-
meter of carbon dioxide, a glittering brass-
bound pump and a filling apparatus. Three
tubs were on the floor containing a blue, a red
and a clear fluid. These, said the Arab pro-
prietor, were English disinfectants in which the
bottles were rinsed. Here you waited until

c

your bottles were refilled, at one anna (one penny) each. This represented a profit of 1,200 per cent. The water which was used for filling them was taken from the centre of the Tigris. Ice was obtained elsewhere, made from an ammonia plant, in bars two feet by six inches. The necessity for ice was imperative, but it could only be supplied in small quantities then. These native plants were mostly taken over by the military as time went on. A single bad heat-stroke case would often use up the whole day's supply to the hospital. That was why ice was an imperative necessity. It meant so many lives saved. In India ice is manufactured by machines in quantity wherever it is required.

After soda water, the sick Tommy requires certain delicacies in food. Eggs and chickens and fruit and vegetables were necessary. The quartermaster soon began to lift up his voice.

CONVOY TIGRIS

A Convoy of Sick and Wounded.

the surface of this cradle of the earth all day in search of certain supplies, returned empty. Chickens and eggs were local produce. The natives put fancy prices on things. What we paid was supposed to be a controlled price. It must be remembered that we introduced a lot of money into the country, and entirely changed the financial standards of the Arabs. Arab coolies got tenpence a day—that is, their pay was not far short of the European Tommy. Sometimes they struck for higher wages. It did not breed a good spirit, but it may have been the best spirit under the circumstances. It was, at times, necessary to use violence to *belumchis*, who insolently demanded absurd charges, and a certain padre gained respect by administering a severe thrashing to one of these rascals. When the Russians came down, one of them was obstructed for a moment by an Arab on the river bank. The Russian officer—

a big fellow—picked him up and threw him into the river.

The chickens were poor. Three might weigh in the aggregate a pound and a half. The supply of eggs was limited when procured through contractors, but it was possible to obtain a few from other sources. As regards fruit, there was practically none. Potatoes were procurable in this part, but not higher up the river. Owing to the intense heat and lack of storage accommodation, vast quantities of food perished. Piles of boxes containing cigarettes, that had lain in the sun, were found to contain nothing but fine dust on being opened. It was the same way with biscuits. Potatoes rotted in millions. The whole problem was one of immense difficulty. The milk that was used was almost wholly tinned. The use of fresh milk which was tried later at Amara was not a very successful experiment. It required forbade alcohol to the people of the country. But then he permitted other things.

Owing to the complaints about food supplies, in the early part of June, in the second year of the campaign, there was published an order that all troops were to have certain fruit and vegetable variations in diet. Lists of articles were given, and the scale was very generous and sensible. The actual supply of the stuff, however, did not come as we might have been led to expect. This was because most of the articles in the lists were starred, which meant that they were only supplied when available, and I suppose India, which had to run several other expeditions besides Mesopotamia, could not possibly produce enough material to satisfy all requirements. At this time, too, many of the cargo vessels were occupied in bringing immense supplies of wood from India, and the local produce of Mesopotamia did not go nearly far enough for the purpose. Some officers planted various seeds in patches adjoining their quarters, but the business of watering them was troublesome. A ration of fresh limes was served to our men on the 21st of June for the first time, but the supply of these ran out the next day. Some of the men retained these small, wrinkled fruits as curiosities. Fish, an intermediate diet for intestinal cases, was sorely missed. But it was quite out of the question. The river fish, of course, were fairly numerous, but the uncertainty of their supply was too great, and they had to be cooked very soon after being caught. There was always a great deal of amateur angling in the evenings, and in the creek by our hospital a kind of mud fish was caught, full of small, apparently unattached bones, and tasting flat and stale.

It is curious to reflect that, in the second

four hundred cases in emergencies. The time they took to travel from the front down to Basra, which is a distance of about two hundred miles, depended very much on the luck they experienced in getting through the Narrows. The passage of this bit of the river will be described in a later page. Three days was a pretty quick journey. Travelling by night was impossible. In rounding the sharp bends of the river, which winds across the plain in a most extraordinary manner, these convoys often cannoned helplessly against the banks. At well-known cannoning places Arabs collected with baskets of eggs and chickens and melons for sale. The sick and wounded lay closely packed on the deck under a single thickness of canvas awning. In the great heat of midsummer this was insufficient protection, but it was impossible for the medical officers of the ships to obtain any extra canvas, and it was thought that reed matting in close proximity to the funnels would be dangerous. Tinned milk for bad cases and bully beef, stew, and bread and jam for those fit to eat it were the main rations, but soup and eggs were often available. The difficulties of catering for a crowded convoy, with only a small galley, were considerable. Water was taken from the river, and chlorinated in tanks on board.

On reaching Basra the convoys discharged their patients either at the big British hospital, that was formerly the palace of a Sheik, and stands on the river's edge, or at one or other of the Indian hospitals that lie beside it. The accommodation for British troops was not great at the time, so that it was the custom to transfer cases as soon as possible into the hospital ships, which could come right alongside the piers, and send them to India. Our hospital no ammunition, no food, and no heart. Hopes ran high, and everyone who came up from Ashar was eagerly questioned. We woke one morning to hear a great noise of steam sirens from the river, and for a time lay in blissful happiness, certain it could only mean one thing. It was like the night we lay on the Gallipoli sand some days after the landing, in the darkness, sipping our first tot of rum. Our hearts were merry, for had we not just heard that Achi Baba had fallen, that Bulgaria and Roumania had declared war on Turkey, and that the crackle of musketry to the north-east was due to certain Boers who were swarming up the heights overhanging the Kishlar Rocks ? She must be a woman of temperament, Rumour, for when she smiles she is so charming; but when she frowns, who can be so ugly ?

During this time considerable activity prevailed throughout the Basra region. Near by, on Makina Plain, a vast flat expanse of bare earth beyond the shadow of the palm plantations, a perpetual dust arose. Transport columns, guns and troops were always on the move, and the camps grew in size until the whole place was dotted with white canvas and yellow matting huts. The skirling of the pipes, the beating of the drums, the sound of the bugle and the tramp of feet continually came from the road that ran along the bank opposite the hospital. Wagons rumbled over the wooden bridge, and the deep note of the incoming steamers reverberated over the groves. But a difficulty began to arise. All these incoming troops that were concentrating on the plain were new to the country. The heat was increasing rapidly. It had long passed the limits of the most intense English summer, and the mercury was now rising above 100 degrees in the shade. The sky was cloudless and brassy. The floods each day left great areas of damp, steamy marsh when the tidal river fell. Mosquitoes were beginning to fill the night with their thin screaming. Small, almost impalpable, colourless insects, whose bite is like a red hot wire and who can penetrate the meshes of an ordinary mosquito net with ease, began to infest the place. These were sand-flies. They are surely the most successfully maddening insect ever designed by the Lord of Flies. They give rise to a malady known as sand-fly fever, which is like influenza and drains the body of all vitality for many days. In addition to this, either the food, the water, the dust, or the day flies were spreading about a form of diarrhœa which rapidly turned into dysentery. The day flies were a swiftly growing army. Breeding grounds in the surrounding camps, in the horse lines, the bullock

The Hospital Washing.

lines and native villages were numerous.   They
were nothing like the flies at Mudros when the
whole roof of a tent at night might be uniformly
black with them, and eating was in the nature
of a free fight.   A couple of hundred or so to
each tent was perhaps the average, but they
made rest a matter of difficulty.   The Red
Cross fortunately supplied us with instruments
of fly destruction, and later on fly experts were
sent out.

The result of all this was that the curve of
sickness began to mount steeply, and it
became necessary to make some provision for
the victims.   Since our position was central
as regards reinforcement camps, we were dele-
gated to deal with local sick, and after that
arrangement very few of the cases sent down
from the front came our way.   For the first
few days the number of incoming sick could be
dealt with adequately.   But as time went on,

IV

HEAT-STROKE

I DO not know of any other malady so
dramatic, or so painful to witness, as heat-
stroke, with the exception, perhaps, of acute
cholera. It is something that belongs to
Mesopotamia in a peculiar sense, in that it
seems to express in visible and concentrated
form the silent hostility of the country which
was noticed by the ancients. For Mesopotamia welcomes no man. It is a profound
enigma. What do those two gigantic rivers
mean that rush through those vast stretches of
barren land ? For what ultimate destiny were

groaning and tossing in the steamy sick tents. The business of getting up is one of infinite weariness. There is nothing fresh in the morning feeling. At eight the mercury is probably 100 degrees. At times, as you dress after a tepid bath, it is necessary to sit down and take a rest. Your vesture is simple—a thin shirt, open at the collar, and a pair of shorts, stockings and shoes. During the day your feelings do not correspond to the height of the mercury, for after breakfast a certain amount of energy possesses you, and the morning's work becomes possible. But after a couple of hours, in the neighbourhood of eleven, when it may be anything from 110 to 120 degrees in the shade, a kind of enervation sets in. This is partly due to lack of food. For some reason we found it necessary to eat a considerable amount. The theory of a simple diet, a little fruit, meat once a day and in small quantity, did not work out in practice. After midday the world is a blinding glare and the intake of air seems to burn the lungs. A comparative stillness descends on the scene. On the plain activities cease. Through the double canvas roofing of a tent the sun beats down like a giant with a leaden club. The temperature in the wards increases. At the worst moments you feel distinctly that it would be possible, by giving way to something that escapes definition, to go off your head. A spirit of indifference to everything is necessary. Any kind of worry is simply a mode of suicide. A man, for instance, who feels continually he ought to be up and doing, and that to lie still in vacancy is a sin, does not do well, unless, perhaps, he dwells in a cool stone house, under fans, with plenty of ice, as was the luck of some. There must be no inner conflicts. Cranks soon suffer. Life becomes simplified. An oriental slapped and punched and laved till they began to turn blue and the temperature fell. Then they were put in a blanket, if any collapse showed, or just left naked on a bed in the open. Fear played a powerful part in the malady. It tended to produce it and to cause relapses, and it was good practice to use direct counter-suggestion whenever the patient was conscious, as well as brandy and morphia. The worst of it was that many of those patients who recovered over night died next afternoon as they lay in the suffocating ward. What was possible with wet sheets and small pieces of ice was done, but it was a wretched business, and those who were in Basra at that time and saw those spectacles will never forget them ; nor will they forget the silent, impotent rage that filled the mind at the thought of the giant-bodied, small-headed Colossus of war which makes a useless sacrifice of men in ways such as these every day. But it had one useful effect, perhaps. A really Zoroastrian reverence for the sun came after seeing a case, and a man learnt to look on his pith helmet and spine pad as his best friends.

E 2

ugly. Forty thousand Arabs were mustering at Kuweit. German cruisers were in the Persian Gulf, sinking shipping right and left. The Turks were coming down on Nasireyah in tremendous force. Trouble was brewing at Shaiba. In the last respect she proved correct, though the trouble was not great. At Shaiba, which lies about twenty miles west of Basra across the plain, a remarkable battle was fought in the April of the year before. A Turkish force of twelve thousand regulars and thirty odd guns, with numerous Arabs, was routed at an extreme and critical moment, it is said, owing to a mistake. The mistake, for once, was on the part of the Turks. Fighting had been very severe. We had no reserves and things were looking black. Numerous Arab tribesmen who had remained as neutral spectators were beginning to take it into their heads that we were losing, and that only means one thing to them.

Donkey Labour in the Heat of the Day.

and began to flee, and the Arabs, changing their minds with incredible swiftness, fell on them in the rear and cut and slashed them about considerably. In the meanwhile the strange column galloped up. But there were no guns. In place of guns stood a strangely assorted collection of wagons, spring carts, tongas— anything on wheels—that a certain doctor had got together and brought up at full speed to take away the wounded. The Turkish Commander, Suleiman Askari, committed suicide.

A New Zealander came into hospital one day from Shaiba way. He was a wireless man, and being so, had found something in the desert that puzzled the science of his mind. He explained the matter. Out there it is a white, undulating expanse, burning hot, but with more air than in Basra. There are extraordinary effects of perspective. A man standing a short way off may assume gigantic proportions, or look like a dwarf. A motor car near by would seem to lose its solidity and dissolve into a few filmy lines. The mirage of water is everywhere. An Arab might lie in the open and no one would see him. A post might look like a horseman at full gallop. It was a country of topsy-turveydom as regards the subjective estimate of the eyes. But what puzzled the wireless man was this. He thought he understood how eye-strain and difference of refractive power of the layers of heated air, or reflected light from the ground and such physical considerations could cause these illusions. But what he could not understand was how it came about that several men would experience exactly the same illusion. Why should a post simultaneously appear as an Arab on horseback or an Arab crawling stealthily on the ground to half a dozen men ? Mirage, like Rumour, is a curious thing. It may have some inner connection

Tommy had to work so hard as those hospital orderlies, and it is not surprising that our casualties in sick men were very heavy. Clerks in the office became ward masters at a moment's notice. But in spite of all this the spirit of the place remained unshaken. However great the heat, it did not destroy that sense of humour which is the glory of the British Army. Rather be beaten and retain that sense than be victorious and lose it. And if you come to think of it, no man who retains his sense of humour is ever really beaten.

VI

THE DAY'S WORK

THE great distances that separate the main stations in Mesopotamia, and the long sea voyage between Basra and Bombay, threw a considerable strain on that part of the army that sits in offices and deals with army forms. At Poona the supreme headquarters of the campaign resided amid the clear breezes of the Indian hills. The consequence was that in cases where two or three copies of a form would have sufficed on the Western front, there it was necessary to multiply them indefinitely, so as to satisfy all the various authorities down the line. For example, in sending sick to India, common effect of this is a " deficient mental energy generally commencing with unnatural drowsiness or loss of appetite and a yearning for stimulants which culminates in that lowering of nerve potential which we know so well as neurasthenia." Thus write the professors of medicine in India on the effects of prolonged heat. I would add to it a large mental element, partly induced by the lack of any kind of amusement, by the want of interest, and by the peculiar effect of a landscape that is entirely flat and uniform. An artificial mountain scenery, painted on canvas, such as one used to see at Earl's Court, would have been a blessed relief. I think a London fog would have been delightful. Towards the end of September, a few small, fleecy clouds appeared one day in the sky and everyone ran out and stared solemnly at them as if they were angels. But there is one phrase that sums up

the prolonged effects of heat better than any
scientific rigmarole. It takes the silk out of
a man.

In Basra there was published daily a small,
excellent newspaper which gave the latest
Reuters and printed selections from papers
that came by the mail. It was sorely missed
when we went up river. I believe it was
edited by a lady. There was a club in Ashar
where it was possible to sit under electric
fans. In old Basra there was an Arab theatre,
containing a few dancing girls and a cine-
matograph. But the arrival of the mails
was the great feature of life out there. They
came roughly once a week, and it is difficult
to describe with what emotions they were
received. The whole district became revivified
for a space under their influence.

Through the month of June the sickness
increased and work went on steadily increas-

were beginning to fall. It had been necessary to surround the hospital clearing with a mud wall, or bund, about four feet in height, in order to keep out the water, for at times there is as much as a six foot rise when the tide comes up the Shatt-el-Arab.

At any simple job of this kind the Arabs are quite good. They can plaster mud on a roof, or make a bund, or run up a mud and reed hut, or raise the level of the flooring of a ward, and they take their time over it. But anything that savours of machinery is usually beyond them. It was a common saying amongst the Arabs that sickness stopped as soon as the dates were gathered in. That proved to be untrue. It was a long while until the dates were ripe, and after they were gathered sickness still continued. The amount of heat those dates required before they turned yellow and soft, and their skins began

On the Shatt-el-Arab near Basra.

ported to hospital rapidly, instead of jolting over the plain in bullock tongas. Unfortunately, the axles of these cars were not quite equal to the rough work, and in a short time they were sent away to other spheres where roads were better. The ground in our neighbourhood was so undermined by floods that on one occasion one of these cars, standing empty, suddenly broke through the upper crust up to its axles. A great deal of perspiration flowed before it was extricated.

In the meanwhile the creek was full of *mahallas* loading up equipment, for we had received orders to go higher up-river.

VII

THE NARROWS

WE left Basra when the Arabs, and the Indian troops, were celebrating the Mohammedan feast of Ramadhan. During the feast, which lasts a month, night is turned into day. No food is allowed, in theory, from sunrise to sunset. Drums beat, dogs howl, cocks crow and the revellers shout and wail and clap their hands in long, rhythmic, staccato periods, and explosions of powder occur under the crescent moon.

A small, double-decked, squat river boat which had been captured from the Turks took us on board. It burned oil fuel. A single and is a small hamlet of white houses. Here there is a wide area of date palms and a great brown, tranquil stretch of river. A white doorway in a yellow wall, shaped like a pear, marks the supposed position of Paradise. The doorway bears a tablet with an Arabic inscription. Behind the doorway, just visible over the wall, a tree grows. This may or may not be the Tree of the Knowledge of Good and Evil, because a dwarfed sinister tree lower down, to which barges tie up, is given the name. But I prefer the one in its walled garden, a faded, simple, harmless - looking tree. And the result of eating its fruit can be moralised on here, for on one side of it is the bazaar square, where whisky and beer and tobacco are sold, and on the other side is the telegraph office with the news of the war blazoned on the iron-studded door and an armed sentry before it.

Beyond Kurna the Tigris takes some immense curves so that at times you seem to see the sails of *mahallas* all round the horizon. We lay on deck, staring idly at the unvarying landscape which quivered under the sun. Occasionally Arab villages were passed, constructed out of the matting made from reeds, which is a local industry. The reeds grow in big patches all the way up the river banks. On the second night we tied up below Ezra's tomb. There was local Arab trouble in this part at the time and we passed an outpost of native troops ; also a mud hut, standing solitary in a swamp in the plain and bearing the words " Leicester Lounge " in black lettering. It seemed deserted.

At night there was a lot of lamp-signalling all round the horizon in naval code. One caught M.M.O. repeatedly and then a lot of figures. Some fires lit up the sky line to the

G

surveyed the plains. He was a kind of police-man, I believe, in our pay. At any rate he seemed to be, like policemen in general, a strong lover of domestic life. Six wives may have contributed a little towards overcoming the extreme monotony of life in the place.

Above Ezra's tomb begin the Narrows. The Tigris becomes very narrow, pouring its filthy yellow water at a great speed between the sharply cut banks. The turns are so sharp, being at times much more acute than a right angle, that the only way to get round is to charge the bank, bump off with a great churning of paddles and creaking of lashings and clanging of the telegraph from the bridge, and work the steamer's nose into the centre of the stream again. The banks, at these spots, are perfectly smooth and polished owing to the constant impacts. By themselves the river steamers could get round more skilfully, but with their clumsy barges on each side it was impossible. The S-boats—the stern wheelers—of which there are only a few, do not carry barges, and therefore their handiness and speed are much greater. They can run from Basra to Sheik Saad, close to the front, within three days, and can travel by night if necessary.

At three in the afternoon as we bumped and scraped and panted up the tortuous river, we came on the familiar sight of a convoy stuck, broadside on, across the river in front of us. A little smoke came from her funnel. The sun beat savagely down on her apparently deserted decks. Behind her there was nothing but shimmering plain and the occasional flash of water. Our engine-room telegraph rang. The engines stopped and we slewed into the bank and dropped anchor. Then the skipper and his navigating lieu-

Pear Drop Reach. But it is necessary to say this with caution, for tampering with great rivers like the Tigris may cause un-thought-of trouble. It upsets the natural balance of the waters.

Gradually the other convoys drew near and dropped anchor above and below the obstructing vessel. Some native troops in one of them got out on the bank and began to bathe, or wandered about looking for fuel to cook their evening meal, and towards evening a string of Arab women and children, from some remote village, came along with eggs and melons and pumpkins. In the meanwhile a kind of activity prevailed in the region of the obstruction. A tug boat appeared and ropes were stretched out to posts on the land and the water was being churned to foam by the paddles. It was said that General Y was on a convoy ahead, and General X, who was going up to replace him, was in a convoy behind us. It was possible to count seven convoys in all, and smoke columns were still rising in the south. It was not until darkness fell that the ship was pulled off, and it was too late to move on that night. So we ate our bully beef and settled down for the night. Once more our sensations were indescribable. The sand-flies were like a million little red-hot wires. There was not a breath of air and the mules screamed and fought and gasped alongside. One hundred and fifty people packed on a small deck, round a funnel that is still burning hot, make a poor job of sleeping in such a climate.

It was the devout prayer of everyone that we might reach our destination next day and get off the ship and away from those mules. That was not to be. We reached

Amara in the darkness of the evening, and anchored near the Rawal Pindi Hospital. Owing to a case of cholera that had developed that day on the starboard barge, we were put in quarantine, so it was necessary to unpack one's kit again and shake down for the night on deck. One of the most refractory mules kicked itself loose of its moorings and fell into the stream in the darkness. Several men risked their lives in rescuing it. One would have thought, seeing that it had been the noisiest and most vicious brute on the barge, that drowning was scarcely good enough for it. And what is a wife to think of her husband when she is told that he was drowned while gallantly attempting to rescue from the swift current of the Tigris a mule that could swim far better than he could? As no one was drowned, perhaps it is unnecessary to ask the question.

VIII

AMARA

WE reached Amara about the middle of July. At that time there was practically nothing happening at the front, but the sickness was great. Amara, by reason of its openness, was a little fresher than Basra, but the temperature was high. It was 125 degrees in the shade on the day following our arrival.

The white low houses line along the river front on the left bank in a more orderly fashion than at Ashar. A bridge of boats connects the two banks. This bridge, which existed before the war, swings open from the centre and lets traffic through. On the right bank a few houses were scattered amongst thick groves of palms. There is somehow a more oriental spirit at Amara than at Basra. The *belums* are more fantastically curved, the mystery of the town more apparent, and the narrow-domed bazaar, full of dim light and vivid colour, is permeated with the spirit of the Arabian Nights. There are some cunning craftsmen in the bazaar, particularly the silver- and gold-smiths, who make exquisite inlaid work. They do this after the manner of true artists, in that they work seemingly more by a process of thought and feeling rather than with the aid of tools. For they sit on the ground with a bowl of water, a small charcoal fire, a strip of metal, and a deeply preoccupied look, and after a time the article is finished. The overlaying of silver by antimony is their particular craft. Owing to the orders they

received, they soon began to charge pro-
hibitive prices.   At certain times it was
possible to get egret feathers, and also astra-
chan—the skin of unborn lambs—in the
bazaar. The old copper vessels that were
sold in many of the shops were sometimes
very beautiful.

The suspected cholera case proving doubt-
ful, we were put out of quarantine next morning, and moved across the river to the site
of the hospital which we were to take over.
It lay round a bend in the river on the right
bank above and well out of the town.   To
the north lay the river, to the south the
desert.   A large number of mud and reed
huts, in long rows, stood on the plain, covering
an area of about a quarter of a square mile.
These were the wards.   There was a sense of
space that was refreshing after the cramped
and littered area of the clearing at Basra,

stabbed by these marauders, who carried long, curved knives, but the main object was looting and not killing.

It was a singular spot to find a large number of women, away up in the heart of that elemental country of fire and water and earth. But they remained untouched by any kind of pessimism, nor were they greatly interested in the campaign as a military affair. All their interest was in their work. They were a wonderful stimulus. Where a man unwittingly tended to let things slide they exhorted and energised. In details, they did not seem to show that gradual decadence that creeps imperceptibly over men when isolated and overworked. It is perhaps so subtle that it takes a woman to detect it. Women may be theoretically unscientific, but they are essential to the maintenance of the scientific spirit and practice. Naturally they suffered sickness,

but not nearly so much as one might have
expected ; for discipline plays a tremendous
part in the avoidance of sickness. It is not
so much a physical factor as a moral one.
It seemed possible to induce a practice of
going sick very easily, and in that climate
it was only necessary to permit some inner
act of surrender that escapes simple definition,
but resembles the lowering of a dog's tail,
and one became a sick man. It was not
exactly malingering.

Beyond the western boundary of the hospital, behind the officers' tents, lay an
oriental garden. An oil engine and pumps
at the river's edge supplied the water to it
through channels. The machine was worked
by an Arab who, as far as one could tell,
prayed to it. In the garden, full of moist
heat and splashes of colour, lived a colony
of jackals, those extraordinary spirits of hell,

their sucking apparatus into the skin. In the morning, what with the sweat and the grease, and the tropical exhaustion, one looked like few things on earth. Oil of citronella is only of temporary use ; paraffin and creosote are of little good. Butter muslin nets are out of the question, as the heat is stifling under them. The burning of aromatic or pungent compounds is useless, and as for killing them, one might lie awake all night, scuffling and dabbing and slapping at the almost invisible forms without gaining the slightest benefit. In the day time they hide in cracks in the ground, under bits of matting or anywhere out of the sun. Sand-fly fever is a malady that begins like influenza. One aches all over. All the side of life that is enjoyment fades away. It is impossible to smoke, or eat, or drink, or read, or talk. In Malta, where it is indigenous, a convalescence

of three weeks is allowed. It was not possible
to allow that in Amara. The fever lasts two
or three days, coming down in two main
stages. The use of opium is recommended.
As regards the use of opium in Mesopotamia,
it was possible to gain the idea from actual
experience that it was a most valuable drug
during the hot season. If limited to three
drugs and no more, for work in that country,
I should prefer opium, Epsom salts and
quinine. The quinine that we obtained through
official channels was in the form of pink
tablets and came from the cinchona plantations at Darjeeling that are run by the
Indian Government. These tablets are coloured pink to prevent fraudulent selling, for
they are handed out to natives in malarial
districts in large quantities, free of charge,
and natives are not great believers in medicine. The tablets are extremely hard and

insoluble.   Prolonged exposure to the action
of dilute mineral acids produces no effect
on them.   We had, for the men, quinine
parades, when five grains were swallowed
as a prophylactic against malaria every day.
They were amusing affairs to watch—serried
ranks with water-bottles, standing to attention while the sergeant dispenser walked with
proper dignity down the line handing a pink
tablet to each man, who gulped it spasmodi-
cally, took a draught of water and returned
to attention.   It reminded one of a religious
ceremony, of some strange communion service.
In giving the quinine in large doses it was
essential to dissolve it, if any effect was
aimed at.   Even then it rarely produced symp-
toms of quinine poisoning.   The home
preparations were more satisfactory to use.
As regards opium, it was useful, apart from
sand-fly fever, in those frayed, sleepless states

of mind that prolonged heat induces. The English idea that a dose of morphia or laudanum at once induces the opium habit, though very safe, is not altogether sound. Other hypnotics were usually not strong enough to give long sleep ; but here, to produce an effect with hypnotics, it seemed necessary to double the dose. This may have had something to do with some deterioration in drugs caused by the big demands of the war. But I do not think it was the only explanation. Of course, for those who dreaded the use of opium, and preferred chloral or bromide, it was only necessary to glance into the tents where the Chinese carpenters slept at night. There one saw rows of comatose figures and if you cared to lift the lips from the gums of those sleepers, you would usually see a little sticky mass of opium wedged in between the teeth. That was one way of solving the problem of sand-flies and heat at night and no doubt an admirable illustration of the dangers of the drug. But it is possible to find illustrations for everything.

At Amara, paratyphoid A was commonest in the troops coming down from the Front. It was not a very grave disorder, but sometimes, particularly when complicated by other factors, it was fatal. It must be remembered that many patients reached us as emaciated skeletons, in the last stage of exhaustion. Special wards were set aside for typhoid cases. Dysentery was also increasing, and wards were reserved for these cases. It was mainly what is called bacillary dysentery, for which Epsom salts is one of the best remedies. All typhoid cases, as soon as convalescent, were sent to India. That was because they often carry the germs in the intestinal tract a long time after recovery and therefore may become a source of infection. They spent on an average three months in India before returning for service. There was no place in Mesopotamia where convalescent patients could be sent with a reasonable prospect of gaining full health. About twenty miles beyond Aligarbi lie the Pashtikhu hills and there in those high altitudes a big military sanatorium might have been established. This would have saved endless transport difficulties, if a light railway had been constructed. But no doubt the military situation rendered the carrying out of such an idea impracticable. Heat-stroke in Amara was common enough, but it did not seem so fatal as at Basra. This, perhaps, was due to the air, which was drier and fresher. The supply of ice was also more adequate.

We had some unlucky spells. It is a curious thing that luck seems to enter into the matter of death rates. I mean that sometimes for two or three days at a time cases seemed to go wrong and die, on the slightest provocation. At other times, when the luck changed, the most hopeless cases would clear up. It was the same way in the operating theatre. It is the same way with everything, whether it be card playing, or business, or war, or love, or thinking, or sport. There are phases in which something seems to overshadow the scene. The direction of the current changes. For a time everything seems to go wrong. The machinery behind life, that is always helping you on, stops and reverses. And there is another aspect of the same thing which doctors sometimes see in a remarkable way. It is the occurrence of similar kinds of cases at the same time. For part of it there is the scientific explanation of infection by germs.

EZRA'S TOMB.

The Shimal was now blowing from the
north-west, bringing the dust in from the
desert. At times it produced a strange effect.
The atmosphere became dun-coloured, thick-
ened at places into opaque and rushing veils.
Under the pressure of the strong, hot wind
the big *mahallas*, with their white sails in
tense curves, careered down the river with
only a streak of white foam under the prow
to show they were not suspended in the air.
The further bank, pale and unsubstantial,
was outlined fitfully in the hurrying gloom.
A kind of lividity spread over the picture,
bleaching it of all colour. Everything in
the wards became silted over with fine powder,
and the big yellow and black hornets and
the long-legged wasps that seem to have two
or three pendant abdomens and are the hue
of Burgundy marigolds, came hurtling through
the unglazed windows to crawl, half-stunned,

about the mud floors. How the ward Sisters anathematised these days! The storms provoked a feeling not unlike east winds at home. They brought out small aches and pains and one got irritable. A thunderstorm would have cleared away the effect, but the sky remained cloudless and brazen.

IX

ARABIAN COMEDY

NOTHING was happening at the front. Occasionally there was spasmodic shelling and bomb dropping, but the heat prevented any general activity. Headquarters was under howitzer fire at times. One shell landed in the mess waiter's tent and damaged nine men.

There was a tale told at the time concerning a powerful Sheik near the front who was neutral. His son becoming ill, he sent to the Turks, and also to us, for a doctor. The Turks, or rather the Germans, sent a German doctor, and a German lady as well, the latter as a bribe. We sent a medical officer, unat-

I

much revered by the Arabs. One can understand, perhaps, how it comes about that fatness is admired in the East. It is so rare. It is much easier to be thin. The sergeant went into hospital for a few days. When he came out he had lost his glory even as Samson was shorn of his strength in a night. His clothes hung about him in huge folds. What had taken him years to produce was lost in six days, and with it went the respect of the Arabs. There is practically no fat in the country. There was no dripping for puddings. The cattle were all lean.

It is necessary to say a word about the Indian *personnel* attached to the hospital. These were the water carriers, washers and sweepers. They had been immensely pleased at the idea of leaving Basra. But at Amara, where they found things little better, there was some lamentation. In temperament they

were mere children requiring a father. But
of one venerable and aged man I would
like to record a few things. He was a gaunt,
tall, grey-bearded fellow as thin as a stick-
insect, and he performed the most menial
of all services, being a sweeper by caste.
But what he did was done with passionate
devotion. He had seen service in France
and spoke a few curious French words.
Troops on active service in France certainly
are taught some strange phrases. All day
he toiled with his kerosine tins and brushes
and when he had nothing to do he invented
something. He would, for instance, dust
the palm trees outside the mess, pausing
always to salute even the shadow of an
officer on the horizon in a stiff cramped
fashion, and then applying himself with silent
zeal to his remarkable task. He came one
day in some grief and said that he had heard

centre lay a fat man, groaning. It was evident
that he was playing a sick part. Beside him
lamented his wife, a dancing girl, squat-nosed
and heavy hipped. The low comedian entered.
It is not in the interests of the public to
describe him too closely. Eventually he
assumed the part of physician. His treatment
of the patient followed the plan of exorcising
a devil. He hit and kicked him, spat on
him and jumped on him. There was no
improvement and the man died. The problem
was now how to bury him. The low comedian
said he would attend to that and heaved
the fat man on his shoulders and went off
to the cemetery. After an interminable pause
he reappeared still carrying the corpse. He
dumped it on the ground and made a gesture
of despair. " It is no good," he said. " I
cannot bury him. I haven't got a pass! "
This brought the house down and the fat

woman woke up and applied herself vigorously to the tambourine. At the theatre at Basra, when European films were shown, the Arabs always laughed very much at the amount of kissing that white folk indulged in. It seemed to strike them as an extraordinary way of passing the time.

Arab women are not beautiful. Their faces are aquiline, their cheek bones high, and their lips coarse. Their figures are lithe and they walk well, with a sinuous swagger. But there is a sharp, harsh tone about them and one could imagine them very accomplished in bitter speeches. Their eyes are their best feature, but they contain an expression that is hard, restless and challenging. They mess themselves about with henna. Some wear nose rings and all wear bangles that clash as they walk. They were interested in the nurses and seemed for some obscure reason him resolutely and the click of a rifle brought her to her senses. Towards the end of August the amount of looting became serious. On the other side of the river was a big camp, where troops were sent to refit and rest. Here the thieves played many cunning tricks and there was some killing. They were adroit in stampeding horses and in the confusion that followed making off with several. The sentries were not allowed to load their rifles, as promiscuous firing was a source of danger to the occupants of the tents, which were crowded together on the plain. At times the looters slipped down the river in boats, and it became necessary to stop all night traffic. Any craft seen during the night was fired at from the bank.

We had our own particular problem. The hospital lay exposed to the plain. A bund, or mud wall, marked the outer boundary.

The native sentries who were allotted to guard the place were insufficient in number, as the area was considerable and thefts were constant.   The doctors and orderlies volunteered to do sentry duty, and one Arab was shot and one wounded.   This did not stop the stealing.   Kit of every kind disappeared.   At times a man woke up to find an Arab calmly removing his mosquito net, while another stood over him with a knife. It was a good policy to remain motionless for a short time.   It was better than remaining motionless for ever.   During the day time a large number of Arab men and women were employed in the hospital area.   There were about fifty or so who sat all day under a matting shelter making mortar by some mysterious process of hammering, singing their eternal nursery rhymes that sound like " Ina Dina Dinah Do " over and over again.   All these Arabs were turned out of the compound before nightfall by the local Arab police —picturesque fellows, who wore khaki uniforms and Arab head cloths—but it is probable that they had something to do with the thefts. They were certainly guilty of other thefts and on one occasion the Indians, who had suffered severely as their tents lay nearest to the plain, very nearly murdered an Arab whom they found with some crusts of bread and some cooking utensils tied up in his clothing.

It seems to be a common belief among some people that the R.A.M.C. orderly is a man with nothing to do. It was an erroneous idea to hold in Mesopotamia, and when we were informed that we could arrange our own guards, there was some resentment. However, there was some chance of an interesting time, so parties were organised to

WALLED VILLAGE ON BANKS OF TIGRIS.

place would have been gutted in a twinkling. On one night a great glare arose from the river and it seemed as if Amara was in flames. A series of tremendous explosions followed. It was an ammunition barge somewhere in the stream that had suddenly blazed up. It was towed away to a safer place, but if the sparks that showered through the air had set fire to any house along the Tigris front, the entire town might have been in ruins by the morning.

During August scurvy was threatening the men at the front. Many Indians went down with it. It is an unpleasant disorder. The gums looked as if they were blown out like little pneumatic tyres. They were reddish-purple, ulcerated, and the stench was oppressive. Hard, woodeny swellings appeared on the legs, and the victim became very decrepit. One of the main preoccupations

THE TIGRIS NEAR KURNA.

in the wards was the differential diagnosis between atypical malaria and typhoid fever, for the malaria that one reads of in text-books did not exist save exceptionally. A man had an irregular temperature for days and it was often extremely difficult to give a name to the cause. Fortunately one had the assistance of a pathological laboratory, where blood could be examined and treated. In general, the typhoid cases were consistently heavy and depressed, while the malaria cases had spells of cheerfulness.

Life in the wards was not so bad for the patients. There was a certain amount of literature—it was never abundant—and there was a gramophone. There was also the occupation of killing flies with a fly-swotter, playing card games and dominoes, grousing, yarning, sleeping and eating. In the cool of the evening, the convalescents would line the river bank and watch the convoys. There was bathing in the river. At times there were rumours of sharks, for sharks go up river as high as Baghdad. It is not possible to go far out in the stream unless one is a very powerful swimmer. The current is very swift. Tortoises used to line the margin of the river in the evening, with their heads sticking out above water, while crowds of angry birds accused them from the wet mud of the shore. Wild duck, partridge, snipe, sand-grouse and doves were fairly numerous, and in the evenings it was possible to get a good bag. It was worth shooting jackals, for their skins were in very good condition. The hospital had a football ground and later on, towards the end of the hot season, a tennis court was made with the aid of a mixture of mud and straw. A cheery innovation was started shortly after the middle of the year. Concert parties, organised in India from the talent of the Army, came out and gave entertainments in the evening, and very good some of them were.

An effort was made to further the interests of medical science, and the Amara clinical society was started at which doctors met weekly and discussed cases and diagnoses, and papers were read. There is, I think, no better proof that, in its central core, medicine is an art, and not a science, than the kind of discussion that goes on at medical meetings. It exactly resembles the discussions that go on in political debating societies. The monotony of life was interrupted at frequent intervals by official inspections. Every General who passed up or down felt it incumbent on him to visit the hospital. A crowd of lean men in khaki, each with what looked like a large collection of stamps on after a long delay, to say that the inspection would be postponed until a later hour.

During September one of the native interpreters came into the venereal tent as a patient. At the time it was under my care. There was, by the way, very little venereal disease amongst the troops, though, of course, the country is full of it. He was a little olive Jewish boy, alert in manner, and muscular, and a good linguist. When war broke out he was living in Baghdad, where he had learned French and English at one of the Mission Schools there, for he was a Christian. When Turkey came in, he fled from Baghdad with many others who wished to avoid conscription. He travelled down the river to Basra. He described the journey as very bad, with little food and a constant fear of being caught. On reaching Basra he heard rumours of our coming expedition, but the most extreme apathy existed in the town. The Turks were indifferent, walking about smoking cigarettes and " making the shoulders to rise a leetle " as they talked. But they kept a watchful eye on the Arabs. When the Turks evacuated Basra a panic ensued. He was living at the time in a merchant's house and they barricaded the doors and windows and got out any weapons they could find. The Arabs from the plains poured into the town and began to loot. They looted the customs house in particular, and other official places. He saw many street fights in the white dust under the glare of the sun, but he said it was usually the Arab looters fighting amongst themselves. Their fights would last a long time, the men circling round one another with knives, or sniping from street corners. There was a great deal of musket firing at night. This state of

British soldiers very well. The officers, oh, yes. But the men, no. There was leetle to eat." Two months later, when things were quieter, he went to a party of Arabs who were going down the river and made an offer. " I did not trust them, so I went to a Christian house and left three pounds there, and then I gave them three pounds and told them if I arrived safely I would write a letter and they could get the other money when they came back." The Arabs, finding no way of doing him in—after much thinking, I suppose —agreed and they set off. They went down the Shatt-el-Hai way, to the Euphrates, and after a lot of trouble, he got through to the British lines, where he resumed his duties as interpreter.

He was a curious mixture of daring and cowardice, like most of the natives in Mesopotamia. He was very pleased with the hospital, but expressed a crafty sentiment. "You have too many hospitals," he said. "The Turks do not have these hospitals, for then all their men would become sick. It is nicer to be in a hospital than in a desert." This thought brings to the memory an incident that occurred in one of the wards. A new case was admitted, and next morning the doctor overhauled him. He found nothing wrong. "Well, what is the matter with you?" "There ain't nothing the matter," was the reply. "You see it's like this, sir. My pal Bill, in my platoon, he was out of 'orspital day before yesterday, and he says: 'Ginger, me boy, if you want a nice bed for ter sleep in, such as you've forgotten the sight of, you go into 'orspital.' So next day I reports myself sick, carrying on a lot and the new doctor what joined us last week, 'e sends me straight 'ere. And they washes

XI

EDEN REVISITED

TOWARDS the end of October the weather became cooler, and in November the nights were chilly. Sickness diminished rapidly. At this season there is a kind of charm about Mesopotamia. Clouds begin to inhabit the skies and the colour effects, especially those of dawn and sunset, are lovely. It is a time intermediate between the season of heat and the season of floods—a brief time, but one in which the country is at its best. Mosquitoes and sand-flies vanish. A lovely bird, a deep blue and russet, sings in the groves. The blue jay screams and darts through the palm-one disadvantage in the produce of this garden—its flavour was rather weak.

Coming down the river at the end of the year the railway was a great new feature of the country. Small tank engines were crawling over the plain and all along the banks were piles of sleepers and gangs of Arabs. We reached the entrance of the Narrows at dusk and anchored for the night. It was a night that differed entirely from those we endured when going up. There was a concert party on board, and a cavalry major who possessed some tomato soup. That night the sky was superb with stars. Taurus rose, with Aldebaran as red as fire ; then Castor and Pollux calm in their symmetry, with the Pleiades above like a shattered diamond. Then glittering Orion slowly swung above the horizon. In the middle of the night there was a crash of musketry, and a sudden uproar.

The major appeared, speaking Hindustani very rapidly, his eyes closed. It appeared that some Arabs had crept on to the barge next the shore and tried to loot some mail bags. Quiet was soon restored. At dawn a crescent moon, upholding Venus at her fairest, hung in the east, throwing a soft white flame over the dark water.

That night we reached Kurna and tied up alongside the Garden of Eden. It was pitch black. A string of little Arab boys suddenly emerged from a brightly illuminated door each with a sack and slipped on board. This was the mail for Basra, from the dwellers in Eden. About nine a dim, white-robed procession passed down the river-side with a lamp, a torch and a beating drum and vanished into a building. A wedding was being celebrated in the Garden of Eden. Next morning that bride of yesterday might have